To/ DAD,

HAPPY FATHERS DAY.

LOVE

Ken x   emily x

DAN   Jon
  x   xxx

CW00695095

WHEN BRITANNIA RULED THE WAVES

THE HEYDAY OF THE ROYAL NAVY

THROUGH THE PAINTINGS OF VICE ADMIRAL
SIR HENRY KITSON, KBE, CB
(1877–1952)

FRANK KITSON

HALSGROVE

First published in Great Britain in 2007

Copyright © 2007 Frank Kitson
Paintings and Photographs © 2007 individual copyright owners

*All rights reserved. No part of this publication may be reproduced,
stored in a retrieval system, or transmitted in any form or by any means
without the prior permission of the copyright holder.*

British Library Cataloguing-in-Publication Data
A CIP record for this title is available from the British Library

ISBN 978 1 84114 597 6

HALSGROVE

Halsgrove House
Bagley Green, Wellington
Somerset TA21 9PZ
T: 01823 653777
F: 01823 216796
email: sales@halsgrove.com
website: www.halsgrove.com

Printed and bound by D'Auria Grafiche Spa, Italy

Contents

ACKNOWLEDGEMENTS

The vast majority of the pictures in this book belong to Admiral Kitson's sons or grand-children. My thanks are due to them for allowing their pictures to be included. I would particularly like to thank Commander T.E.R. Kitson, Royal Navy, retired, not only for allowing his pictures to be used, but also for the immense amount of trouble he has taken in explaining their background and significance. My thanks are also due to Simon Butler and his staff at Halsgrove for their great skill in sorting and arranging the large number of pictures and fitting them all together.

Also acknowledged are the Imperial War Museum for permission to use the photograph of Admiral Fisher in his cabin which appears in the 1992 Folio Society's version of *Pax Brittanica* by James Morris, originally published in 1968 by Faber & Faber. The photographs of HMS *Calcutta* on p 62 and 79, and the photograph of HMS *Cornwall* on p.79 are from the Halsgrove archives. The engraving of *Britannia* as a hulk on p.86, by W.L Wyllie, was given to HK's wife on leaving Portsmouth in September 1955.

ALSO BY FRANK KITSON

Gangs and Counter-gangs
Low Intensity Operations
Bunch of Five
Warfare as a Whole
Directing Operations
Prince Rupert, Portrait of a Soldier
Prince Rupert, Admiral and General at Sea
Old Ironsides, The Military Biography of Oliver Cromwell

HMS Lion, *Vice Admiral Beatty's flagship at Jutland, 1916.*
(pastel 2′5″x1.2″, 1949)

Portrait of Vice Admiral Sir Henry Kitson by Guy Lipscombe, painted at Falmouth, 1941.
(oil on canvas 2'4"x2'1")

INTRODUCTION

From the time the guns fell silent at Trafalgar, few doubted that Britannia ruled the waves. She continued to do so throughout the 19th Century, although several other countries maintained strong fleets. By the 1880s both Russia and France seemed to be a threat to her supremacy and Britain started to enlarge the Royal Navy. The next challenger was Germany whose attempt to share the sovereignty of the seas, resulted in a massive acceleration in the enlargement and modernisation programme: more and better ships were built at breakneck speed.

In practice naval supremacy depends on many things such as the number and capability of the ships, the standard of leadership, training and morale, the capacity of the dockyards and the whole business of procurement and logistics. But perhaps the easiest way of demonstrating the extent of naval expansion is to look at its manpower. Between 1890 and l910 the strength ofthe Royal Navy virtually doubled from 67,000 men to 131,000. In the war that ensued, it shot up again so that by 1918 it had reached a figure of around 450,000. By the end of that year Germany and Russia were both defeated, France was an exhausted ally and no one was threatening Britannia's supremacy at sea.

Between the wars the size of the Royal Navy dropped, but by 1939 it was back to the strength it had been in l910. By 1945 its strength had risen to 850,000, but by then it was sharing the sovereignty of the seas with the navy of its great ally, the United States. It is impossible to know at what point Britannia ceased to rule the waves, but within a few years Uncle Sam was brandishing her trident. Thereafter the Royal Navy shrunk so that now (2007) it numbers slightly less than 40,000, although still the second largest navy in the world in terms of tonnage. Naturally its size and shape is tailored to the tasks likely to confront it and the threats facing it. on the other had its health varies from time to time according to the resources it receives.

This book is about a youth who joined the Royal Navy in 1891 and left it at the age of sixty-five in 1942, nine months after the United States entered the second world war. In addition to being a successful officer who rose to high rank he was from his early days a beautiful artist. This book consists of a written account of his career illustrated by his paintings and a number of photographs mainly from his own albums.

The book is divided into three parts. Each part starts with a written account illustrated with selected paintings and photographs, followed by the main collection of paintings and photographs relevant to the period concerned.

Frank Kitson
2007

PART I
1891–1910

Nowadays the golden years of Queen Victoria's reign appear to us as ancient history, although thanks to endless films and television programmes, Hitler's war seems almost part of the world in which we live. To that extent Kitson's life spanned the gap between history and the post war world. The purpose of this book is first to display the quality and variety of his artistic ability and second to give an idea of what life for a naval officer was like at that time. For convenience sake the first part of the book deals with Kitson's experiences in the navy of Victoria and Edward VII. The second covers his activities during the first, or Great War as it was then known, including the preparatory period and its aftermath. The third covers the inter-war years and the Second World War.

Henry Karslake Kitson was born 22 June 1877 at Western House outside Highweek Village near Newton Abbot, Devon, the elder son and third child of Major Edward Kitson recently retired from the Indian Army. The family had long been resident in Devon and several cousins lived nearby on Dartmoor. As a result he was able to spend much of his childhood there, fishing and collecting butterflies and birds' eggs. After schooling at Newton College he joined HMS *Britannia* as a cadet in 1891, following in the footsteps of his mother's brother, Comyns Karslake, a serving captain in the Royal Navy. Kitson's subsequent naval career spanned a period of fifty-one years. From the start he was active as a painter and he continued to produce pictures until his death ten years after he retired from the navy.

In 1891 when Kitson joined the Royal Navy as a cadet, the two hulks *Britannia* and *Hindustan*, were moored end to end in the Dart estuary where they stayed until the Britannia Royal Naval College was built to take on the role of training naval cadets about ten years later. He joined at a good moment. Concern for the growing strength of the French and German navies had been causing unease in the country. As a result, two years earlier Parliament had passed the Naval Defence Act, which enshrined the principle that the Royal Navy should always be as strong as the next two navies in the world added together. This gave rise to a rapid increase with many new warships being built. Further impetus to the building program arose from Germany's challenge to England's supremacy at sea during the early1900s. There is nothing like belonging to an outfit that is growing and in the first twenty years of his service, the Royal Navy doubled its strength.

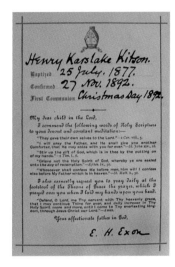

Certificate of confirmation by the Bishop of Exeter.

Group photograph of cadets who joined Britannia *with H.K. in 1891.*

The hulks Britannia *and* Hindustan *moored end to end in the River Dart.*

Prince Louis of Battenberg, Captain of HMS Cambrian.

At the age of sixteen, Kitson was appointed as a midshipman to HMS *Empress of India*, a large battleship in the Channel Squadron. The ships of this squadron moved around the south and west coasts of the British Isles and as far afield as Gibraltar. At the end of 1894 he joined HMS Cambrian, a cruiser in the Mediterranean Fleet, in which he served for the next year. This was followed by two years in HMS *Calypso* a square-rigged ship with an auxiliary engine, which was part of the Training Squadron. At the time she was classed as a 16 gun screw cruiser, 3rd class, but displacing no more than 2,770 tons she was really no more than a corvette. The purpose of the Training Squadron was to give junior officers and ratings a thorough grounding in seamanship. The squadron sailed south as far as Gibraltar and north to Iceland and Norway.

During his service as a midshipman he had not only experienced life on board three very different kinds of warship, but he had met many of the people with whom he would be working over the next forty years. Amongst these, it is of interest that his captain in Cambrian was Prince Louis of Battenburg, who became First Sea Lord at the start of the Great War. A fellow midshipman in *Calypso* was Dudley Pound who was First Sea Lord at the start of the Second War.

Whilst still at school Kitson had shown promise as an artist but it was during his early years at sea that the pictures with which he illustrated his log, show how far he had developed at an early age. All midshipmen, who were at the bottom of the tree so far as naval officers

Left: *HMS Calypso, broadside on (an illustration in log), 1896.* Above: *Cover of H.K.'s first log and endplate illustrating his second log.*

were concerned, had to keep a log which was inspected by a supervising officer and periodically by the captain. His pictures, of ships, maps, rigging, gun turrets and guns, are not only of artistic interest but also bring the Royal Navy during the closing years of Queen Victoria's reign very much to life. There are battleships and cruisers and some of the few remaining sailing ships still in commission at the time, together with a number of foreign warships and merchantmen.

While still serving in HMS *Empress of India*, Kitson had sent some pencil sketches of ships taking part in the fleet exercises of 1894 to the Graphic newspaper. Although newspapers were by now printing some photographs, they still relied to a considerable extent on draw-

HMS Calypso, *head on.*
(Log)

H.K.'s first ship, HMS Empress of India, *1894.*
(Log)

A sketch sent to the Daily Graphic *magazine showing fleet manoeuvres in 1894.*

ings sent in by artists to illustrate the news and current affairs. The sketches that he sent in 1894 were the first of many that he sent to the *Graphic* and the *Illustrated London News* over the coming years.

On leaving *Calypso*, Kitson spent some months on training courses before qualifying as a sub-lieutenant. He then spent a short time in torpedo boat destroyers. Torpedoes had been introduced into the Royal Navy in the 1870s and were designed to be launched from small craft described as torpedo boats. The threat posed by these boats was countered by the development of torpedo boat destroyers, soon to be known as destroyers. They were small, fast and very uncomfortable in a heavy sea. Remembering his time in them many years later, he said that on one occasion he was the only man on board who was not sea-sick.

His next appointment was to HMS *Renown*, flagship of Vice Admiral Sir John (Jackie) Fisher, Commander-in-Chief of the North America and West Indies Station. Jackie Fisher was the ruthless moderniser whose reforms were largely responsible for getting the navy fit to fight in the Great War. He was regarded as a tiger and much feared by his captains. But he had

Torpedo Boat Destroyer
(Log)

H.K. as a sub-lieutenant with Royal Marine, 1897.

Three pencil sketches of Torpedo Boats travelling at speed.
(Sketch book)

Admiral Jackie Fisher in his cabin on board HMS Renown, *his flagship in North American and West Indies station 1897–1899. The date of the photograph is not known but as Fisher was promoted to full Admiral in 1901 is was taken before that date, possibly when* Renown *was at Plymouth between two stations, late 1899.*

The older woman is probably Lady Fisher whom he married in 1866.

a great sense of fun and was well liked by the junior officers, and ratings. Jackie Fisher had his wife and three daughters with him. Kitson joined the ship in Halifax, Nova Scotia, in September 1898, and went down the St Lawrence in her as far as Quebec, before sailing to Bermuda. During this cruise the Admiral's horses and carriage were embarked as well as some cows to provide his family with fresh milk.

HMS *Renown* was a new first class battleship of 12,350 tons with a main armament of 10in guns, first commissioned in 1897. It was to be Kitson's home for almost the next three years. When the fleet was at Bermuda, the Admiral lived ashore and frequently invited the officers to his house for parties. At Christmas the whole family came on board and went round the mess decks when the men were having their Christmas dinners. The eldest daughter was a keen artist and on occasions Kitson found himself detailed off to take her to some scenic spot where they could do some sketching. Early in 1899 *Renown* left for a further cruise around the West Indies to Jamaica. Not long after returning to Bermuda she sailed for England with the Admiral who had been appointed Commander-in-Chief of the Mediterranean Fleet. After a few weeks leave the ship sailed for the Mediterranean arriving in mid-July.

HMS Renown

Life in the Mediterranean Fleet was more hectic than at Bermuda as one major exercise followed the next, interspersed with visits to foreign ports and return visits by French, Italian and Turkish ships. When in port there were many sporting competitions between the different ships, Kitson excelling at cricket and hockey. Sometimes he and one or two friends would get away for a few days fishing or partridge shooting. In October 1900 he was promoted to the rank of lieutenant. On one occasion when there was a dance on board, Jackie Fisher told Kitson that he was to ask the captain of the ship for a dance and when the captain refused he was to jump overboard in all his mess kit. He did so and was hauled aboard in a bedraggled condition with the captain fuming and Fisher laughing as he gave him a cheque to buy himself a complete new mess kit. After almost three years he left the *Renown* in August 1901. As the merchant ship carrying him home left harbour, the *Renown*'s band fell in and played Auld Lang Syne, a gesture that he greatly appreciated.

It was now time for him to undergo a prolonged series of training courses at Greenwich, after which he did further courses and visits to qualify as a specialist in torpedoes. By June 1903 he was posted as an instructor on the staff of HMS *Defiance*, a training ship at Plymouth. He detested the courses but greatly enjoyed his time in Defiance during which he and a few other officers got the shooting rights over 300 acres in Cornwall where they were able to enjoy themselves over the coming winter. In the late summer of 1903 he was attached to HMS *Hawke* during the massive manoeuvres involving the Home, Channel and Mediterranean Fleets which he found to be highly instructive. The Captain of *Hawke* was

HMS Hawke, *watercolour, 1894.*
(Log)

Sir George Warrender with whom he seemed to get on remarkably well, as a result of which he found himself appointed in the following year to Sir George's next ship, HMS *Lancaster*, a new 1st class cruiser of 9,000 tons. One year later in mid-1905 he was back in HMS *Renown* as the Torpedo Specialist and as No 2 to the First Lieutenant.

At this time the *Renown* was in dock being prepared to take the Prince of Wales, later to become King George V, for a lengthy tour of India, Burma and Ceylon. When all was prepared the ship sailed to the Mediterranean, taking the Prince and his wife on board at Genoa on 20 October. *Renown*, with her royal passengers embarked, met the Mediterranean Fleet at sea and was escorted by these great ships for some distance. Kitson recorded and sketched these manoeuvres, sending the results to the *Illustrated London News*. The *Renown* then passed through the Suez Canal, arriving at Bombay on 9 November.

The voyage had enabled the officers to get to know their Royal passengers. Kitson started well by making a grand slam in no trumps when partnering the Prince at bridge and his

HMS Renown *at the time of the Prince of Wales' visit to India.*

Left: The ship's company of HMS Renown *with the Prince and Princess of Wales. Right: Their Royal Highnesses, the Prince and Princess of Wales on board HMS* Renown.

sketches were a source of interest to both the Prince and Princess of Wales. A less pleasurable aspect of the trip was the fact that, as Torpedo Officer, he was in charge of much of the ship's electrical fittings, as the specialist electrical branch of the navy had not yet been set up. In this capacity he not only had to devise and assemble strings of coloured light bulbs to be hung between the masts when the ship was illuminated for special occasions, but also to provide extra fans and a light over the shaving mirror in the royal apartments at short notice.

On arrival in India the Prince and Princess moved around largely by train but rejoined the ship from time to time at different ports. On occasions Kitson managed to spend a considerable time on shore. He was particularly interested in visiting the Indian Mutiny battlefields at Delhi and Lucknow, particularly as his father as a young officer had taken part in the campaign. He made a number of paintings of these places and also some of scenery in Burma and Ceylon as the tour progressed. Not until March 1906 did the ship with the Royal Party leave for home.

During this voyage Princess Mary said that she would like his picture of the Taj Mahal so he made a copy and let her chose which of the paintings she most liked: she chose the second one. On returning through the Suez Canal *Renown* again met up with the Mediterranean Fleet near Crete and prepared to welcome King Edward VII who arrived in the Royal Yacht on 11 April, together with the Queen and Princess Victoria. Thereafter there was a further round of visits to the Piraeus and Corfu during which meetings took place with the King of Greece and various members of the Greek Royal Family. During the course of the many dinner parties, picnics and inspections Kitson met the King and most

The Residency at Lucknow where H.K.'s father fought during the Indian Mutiny.
(Watercolour 10"x8")

The waterfront, Bombay.
(Watercolour 9.5"x6")

The Taj Mahal from Agra. One of two pictures of this scene painted by H.K., the other being presented to HRH Princess of Wales.
(Watercolour 14"x10")

of the other exalted persons. Two weeks later *Renown* headed back to England arriving at Portsmouth in early May when the Prince and Princess of Wales left the ship for the last time. An odd post-script to the tour was that Kitson's father actually left Devon to see the ship arrive back. Having been taken round the ship he returned home the same afternoon, saying that he did not like to be away for more than a day. Although he lived for a further 31 years, there is no record of him ever again leaving the county.

Thereafter *Renown* was reduced to a skeleton crew under the commander and remained in the dockyard until the end of July when she went to Cowes as the guard ship for the Regatta. There followed a further series of visits from high ranking persons including the Prince of Wales, the King and Queen of Spain, Prince Louis of Battenburg and Jackie Fisher. At the end of the Regatta, *Renown* returned to Portsmouth dockyard and paid off. Kitson went on a refresher course in the *Vernon*.

His next appointment was as first lieutenant and torpedo officer of HMS *Hyacinth*, a 2nd class cruiser completed in 1901. She was the flagship of the newly promoted Sir George Warrender, commander-in-chief of the East Indies Station, based at Colombo. It was a bit of a backwater and he spent the next two and a half uneventful years in the seas and ports of the Indian Ocean Persian Gulf and Western Pacific. It was at this time that he started to catch and paint a series of watercolours of sea fish. Eventually there were a hundred different species illustrated in this collection. It was also at this time that he received the medal of the Bombay Art Society for his paintings, some of which he exhibited and sold for a considerable amount of money. He was to receive another such medal in 1914.

HMS Renown *alongside at Madras.*

Cricket team from HMS Hyacinth. *H.K. seated third from left*

Battleship HMS Centurion, 1893.
(Log)

PAINTINGS & PHOTOGRAPHS
1891–1910

The paintings, drawings and photographs appearing in this section illustrate the period 1891-1910 and are taken from journals and other sources from this time.

Top: *Frontispiece from H.K.'s logbook from HMS* Empress of India.

Left: *A watercolour in H.K.'s log in October 1893 of HMS* Victory *going into action.*

Below: *Six Midshipmen from HMS* Empress of India *together with the Flag Lieutenant and a Warrant Officer. H.K. centre, sitting.*

A track chart from H.K.'s log showing the passage of HMS Empress of India *from Plymouth to Gibraltar.*

Four watercolours from H.K.'s Midshipman's log done in the period 1893-1897.

HMS Blenheim

HMS Bellanot

HMS Rodney

Dartmouth trawler

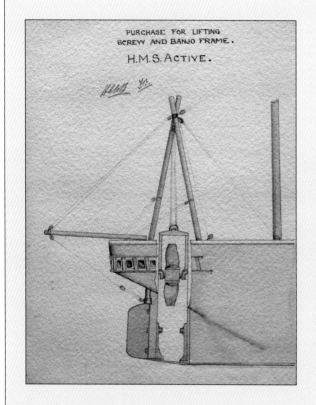

PURCHASE FOR LIFTING
SCREW AND BANJO FRAME.

H.M.S. ACTIVE.

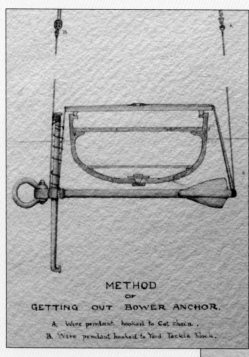

METHOD
OF
GETTING OUT BOWER ANCHOR.

A. Wire pendant hooked to Cat chain.
B. Wire pendant hooked to Yard Tackle block.

Further watercolour illustrations from H.K.'s Midshipman's log showing ways of carrying out a variety of functions at sea, as described. These are drawings of great accuracy and precision. Each is signed by H.K. and countersigned by an officer.

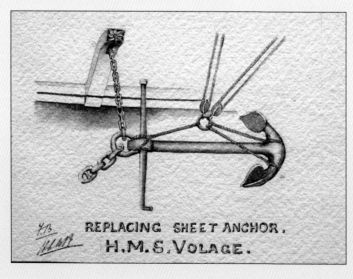

REPLACING SHEET ANCHOR.
H.M.S. VOLAGE.

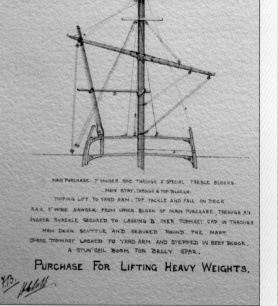

PURCHASE FOR LIFTING HEAVY WEIGHTS.

Pen and wash drawing of Palma Cathedral.
(Log)

Below: *An anchor as decoration for anchor bearings. These give the bearings from the ship to three prominent features ashore to establish the ship's position while at anchor. Similar pictures appear throughout H.K.'s logs.*

Small watercolour of a square-rigged vessel off the coast, 1894.

LAS PALMAS.

ANCHOR BEARINGS.

Castle.	S 89° W.
Watch House.	N 8° E.
Citadel.	S 34° W.

Watercolour illustration of the cruiser HMS Grafton, 1895. This is reproduced at the same size as it appears in the log where all pictures have to fit in the page size 12"x8". Usually there are several small pictures on each page.

When promoted to sub-lieutenant there was no further requirment on H.K. to maintain a log. He thereafter kept a private journal which he illustrated. This watercolour is of a cruiser in the US Navy, the USS Marblehead, *and dates from 1899.*

Painting of the Training Squadron at sea. H.K. served in HMS Calypso *of the squadron 1886–1897.*
(Watercolour 20.5"x12.5")

A full page painting from H.K.'s journal of a square-rigged ship escorted by a tug, dating from 1899.

Left: Two pencil drawings from H.K.'s sketchbook.

Full page painting from the log of an unidentified cruiser.

Portland - illustrated in the log, 1894.

Full page painting of an eighteenth century frigate, 1894. Pencil drawing (below) *of French battleships.*
(Log)

These two illustrations of fleet manoeuvres of 1894 were reproduced in the Daily Graphic from sketches sent by H.K. In the accompanying note in his sketchbook H.K. refers to 1893, although the manoeuvres took place in the following year.

The battleship HMS Ramillies, *from log, 1895.*

Small sailing boat off Algiers, from log, 1895.

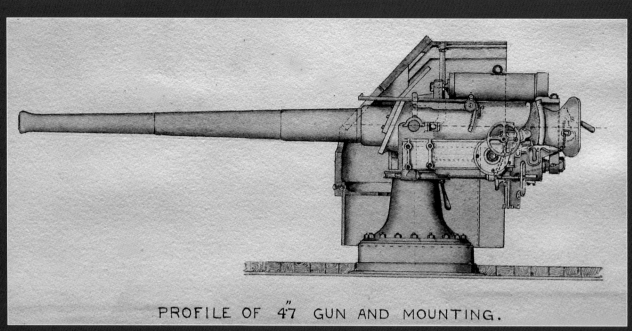

Full page diagrammatic drawing from log of a 4.7-inch gun and mounting, 1895.

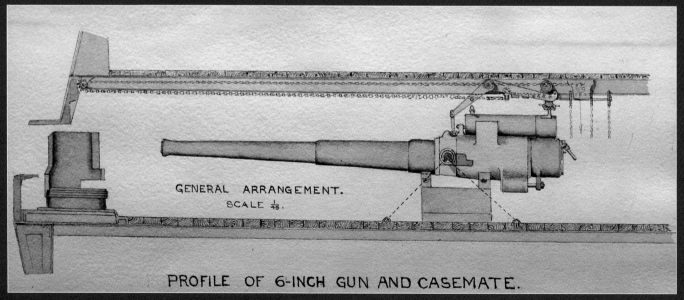

Full page diagrammatic drawing from log of a 6-inch gun and casemate, 1895.

HMS Cambrian. *A full page painting from the log, 1895.*

Small painting of HMS Cambrian *from log, 1895. H.K. was serving aboard her at this time.*

HMS Speedwell, *and (inset) the Russion ship* Razboynik.
(Log)

An elderly battleship HMS Sans Pariel, *1895.*
(Log)

Italian battleship Umberto, *1895 and (inset) below HMS* Champion.
(Log)

Italian battleship Stromboli.
(Log)

Full page painting of a merchant ship from Bermuda, with a paddle steamer in foreground, 1899.
(Journal)

Opposite page, clockwise from top left: *HMS* Renown, *Bermuda, 1899.* USS Indiana, *1899,* SS Carthaginian, *1895 and Austrian battleship* Monarch *in the Mediterranean, 1899.*
(Journal)

HMS Renown in port, 1899
(Watercolour 9"x14")

HMS Renown at sea, 1899
(Watercolour 11"x8")

The Mediterranean Fleet at sea, 1899.
(Watercolour 11"x9")

Two watercolours of inhabitants of northern Norway, painted when the Training Squadron visited the area in 1896.

Watercolour of the Spanish Port, Bermuda. Full page painting from H.K.'s journal, 1899.

Mediterranean scene. Full page painting from the journal, 1899.

These two paintings, were created by H.K. while a midshipman in the mid 1890s.

H.K. started doimg character sketches of his acquaintances around 1900, stopping in 1908 when he discovered they were having an affect on his personal relationships. The four shown here are given as examples of the styles he used.

The photograph shows a group of lieutenants attending Royal Naval College, Greenwich in 1902. H.K. is third from left of those standing in the front row.

The two watercolours here date from the tour of India by the Prince and Princess of Wales 1905–06.

Above: *The Red Fort at Agra.*
(Watercolour 8"x8.5")

Right: *Myritkina on the banks of the Irawaddy*
(Watercolour 8"x8.5")

The photograph shows officers on board HMS Hyacinth *1907-09. H.K. is second from left, middle row.*

Above:
*The ship's company
of HMS* Hyacinth.

Above right:
*Ordinary Seaman
from HMS* Hyacinth.

Right: *Large water-
colour of seafront at
Bombay. This was
painted by H.K. in
1909 and sold. It
was rediscovered in
the 1960s in a shop
in England and
bought back by the
family.*

Left: *H.K. with his brother Edward (Ned) aged 18, and his father Edward, aged 66, 1906.*

Right: *H.K. with his sister, Edie, 1906.*

The scene from the Bovey Tracey–Lustleigh road looking towards Hay Tor Down, in Devon painted by H.K. in 1909.
(Watercolour 10"x4")

PART 2
1910–1921

At the end of his time in the East Indies Kitson returned to home waters and joined the battleship HMS *Bulwark*, flagship of the Vice Admiral commanding two of the divisions of the Home Fleet. For the next four years up to the start of the Great War the Royal Navy experienced a period of accelerating reorganisation and reinforcement. In particular the various fleets and squadrons in home waters organised originally to fight the French, combined to form what was known as the Home Fleets consisting of the First, Second and Third Fleets in which were most of the country's capital ships. On the understanding that France would take the lead in the Mediterranean our fleet there was greatly reduced. Of the Home Fleets, the First was fully manned, the Second was manned by a strong cadre which could be brought up to full strength within a few days of mobilisation and the Third was unmanned and would take up to a month to be ready for war. *Bulwark* was in the First Fleet. After eighteen months *Bulwark* paid off and Kitson together with the rest of her crew transferred to HMS *Africa* which took on the role of flagship.

In August 1911 he became first lieutenant of HMS King *Edward VII*, flagship of the Second Fleet, and six months later on promotion, he became the commander and executive

HMS King Edward VII *at anchor. When launched in 1903 by King Edward VII in person, he decreed that she would always be a flagship.*

Officers of HMS Highflyer. *H.K. third from left in second row.*

HMS Highflyer *which sank a German armed merchant cruiser in the early months of the Great War.*

officer of the ship; an unusual progression occasioned by the untimely death of his predecessor. After a further six months the crew transferred to HMS *Queen*, a newer battleship carrying out the same function. The idea was that at the start of the war the First Fleet of four battle squadrons would form the basis of the Grand Fleet. The Second and Third fleets were intended to combine and give the Admiralty a pool of older ships, independent of the Grand Fleet, which could be used for other tasks.

In January 1913 after four years in home waters, he was appointed commander of the flagship of the East Indies Squadron, a Plymouth built cruiser named HMS *Highflyer*. Six months later *Highflyer* was replaced as flagship by HMS *Swiftsure*, a battleship first commissioned in 1904, in which he was to spend the next two and a half years as commander and executive officer. At this time an important concern for the East Indies Squadron was the situation in the Persian Gulf where unrest threatened Britain's monopoly of maritime commerce and incidentally her responsibility for maintaining the buoys and lights throughout the area. Kitson looked back on the extreme heat and discomfort of his time in the Persian Gulf with no great pleasure.

At midnight on 4 August 1914 England found herself at war with Germany and the East Indies Squadron's prime task was to find and destroy enemy warships bent on the destruction of English merchantmen. It is interesting to recall that soon after the commencement of hostilities, *Highflyer* engaged and destroyed the German armed merchant cruiser Kaiser *Wilhelm der Gross.*

Turkey's decision to enter the war as an ally of Germany in November 1914 completely altered the strategic situation in the Mediterranean and East Indies. As a result *Swiftsure* and her sister ship HMS *Triumph* were ordered to move to the Suez Canal to support the troops repelling a Turkish attack on Egypt. In January 1915 two Turkish columns attempted to cross the canal north and south of the Great Bitter Lakes. *Swiftsure* played an important part in fighting off these attacks and Kitson was mentioned in despatches by the army commander for his part in the main battle, which occurred on 2 February 1915.

By now Russia was having difficulty in facing heavy German attacks along her Western borders while being assaulted by the Turks from the south. She accordingly begged the English government to take some of the pressure off her by attacking the Turks. It was in this context that Britain moved a number of ships into the Aegean Sea for the purpose of forcing their way through the Dardanelles into the Sea of Marmora, from where they would be in a position to threaten the Ottoman capital of Constantinople. *Swiftsure* and *Triumph* were ordered to join this force which by March consisted of 13 battleships, including a number that Kitson had known in the old Second Fleet, one battle cruiser and a number of cruisers, destroyers, minesweepers and submarines. The French also provided four battleships and some destroyers.

The *German armed merchant cruiser* Wilhelm der Gross.

Left: *The paper recording H.K.'s mention in despatches by the Army Commander, signed by Winston Churchill.* Centre: *HMS* Harding, *a cruiser which played a part in repelling the Turkish advance on Suez Canal.* Right: *HMS* Swiftsure *in the Suez Canal firing on the advancing Turkish force.*

Map of the Gallipoli Theatre of War.

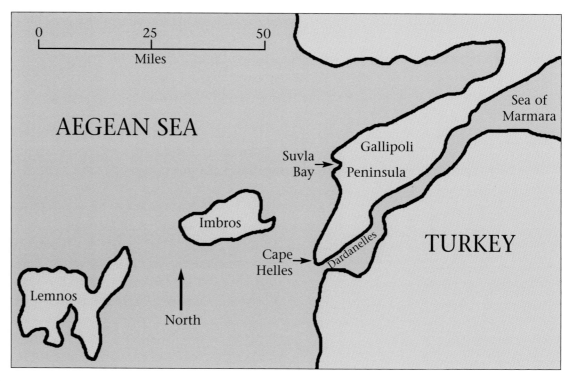

H.K. as Commander of HMS Swiftsure.

On 2 March, the day after her arrival, *Swiftsure* was detailed off to bombard Turkish forts at the mouth of the Dardanelles, which naturally returned the fire. One enemy shell went through the quarterdeck and exploded in the wardroom, wrecking it. This action set the pattern for further bombardments designed to facilitate the move of the fleet through the narrows when the main operation started. The ships usually failed to do much damage to the forts because Turkish minefields prevented them from getting close enough to do the job properly. And because the ships could not suppress the enemy's fire effectively, the minesweepers had difficulty in getting rid of the mines. Soon afterwards on 5 March, *Swiftsure* and *Triumph* together with the cruiser *Euryalus* and a few smaller ships were sent to attack the Turkish port at Smyrna (now Izmir) in an attempt to prevent the enemy using it to interfere with ships moving through the Aegean Sea. *Swiftsure* was involved in bombarding the coastal defences while the smaller ships went close to the harbour to cause as much damage as they could. Swiftsure returned to the fleet outside the Dardanelles on 16 March having called in at Lemnos, which was the base for the forthcoming operations. On 18 March the fleet tried to force its way through the Dardanelles to the Sea of Marmora.

This is not the place to describe in detail the disastrous battle that occurred on 18 March. The general idea was that the battleships would advance in divisions of five ships and fire at Turkish positions while minesweepers cleared the way for an advance by the next division of battleships which would cover further mine sweeping. Suffice it to say that matters did not turn out as intended. It soon became apparent that the guns of battleships could not neutralise the Turkish forts and field artillery to the extent necessary for the minesweepers to fulfil their tasks and the operation was called off.

Throughout the operation *Swiftsure* played her part, entering the straits with the second division of battleships in the early afternoon. Soon afterwards Kitson saw an immense explosion on a French battleship, which went down within about three minutes. Later *Swiftsure*, the rear ship of her division, passed close to the *Inflexible*, which had been badly damaged but which later managed to rejoin the force. At about 4 pm *Irresistible*, next in line to *Swiftsure*, was mined or torpedoed and soon afterwards *Inflexible* was again damaged and had to withdraw for good. Two hours later HMS *Ocean*, flagship of the division, was sunk. It seems that although most of the damage was done by mines, most of the casualties were caused by Turkish gunfire as the crews were being rescued. As it got dark the whole fleet was withdrawn to an anchorage outside the straits. *Swiftsure* had been lucky. With ships disabled or sunk all round her, she had sustained no more than superficial damage, but throughout the night her crew were busy taking on board survivors and generally helping ships that were worse off than herself.. The net result of the day's fighting was three battleships lost, several others severely damaged and the whole fleet back where it started.

It was now decided to land an army to force the Turks off the Gallipoli peninsula, which

Pencil sketch of troops being towed towards the Gallipoli Peninsula, drawn by H.K. at the time of the landings, 24 April 1915.

A second pencil sketch of the landing at Gallipoli, 1915.

formed the northern shore of the straits and capture the forts. This would enable the navy to sweep the mines and sail the fleet through to the Sea of Marmora. An army of British, Australian and New Zealand troops, some 70,000 strong, was therefore assembled and an invasion launched across a front of about ten miles over a number of beaches at the end of the peninsula on 24 April. But by this time six divisions of the Turkish Army, aware of the danger, had reinforced the defences and were ready to repulse the invaders.

Before dawn troops were brought to a point off the beaches in cruisers or merchant ships and there transferred into ships' boats. A number of these boats were then towed to the shore by motor launches commanded by midshipmen and landed on the beach. In one case a specially prepared collier, the famous *River Clyde*, was run up the beach and the soldiers disembarked directly onto the shore. This was at V beach, in the very mouth of the straits. Just to the north was W beach where the Lancashire Fusiliers made their historic landing and to the north of that again were X and Y beaches. *Swiftsure* was one of the battleships giving covering fire off X and W beaches and was credited with completely subduing the opposition at X beach. The landings which took three days to complete succeeded, but at a considerable cost in lives. Thereafter the battleships continued to give supporting fire to the army as it pushed inland, frequently using naval seaplanes to report the fall of shot. Kitson himself went up in a seaplane on several occasions and made a number of sketches of the ground over which the soldiers were fighting. None of the battleships was lost during the landing operations, although most were hit by Turkish artillery.

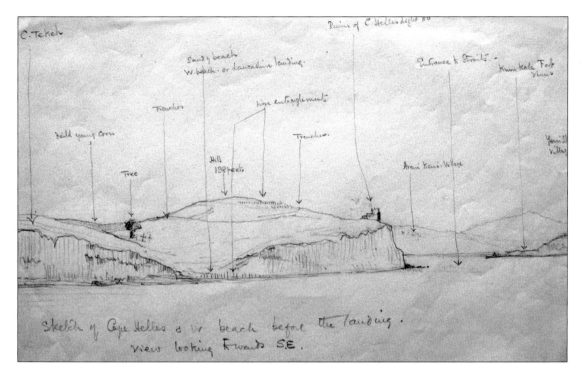

Pencil sketch of the mouth of the Dardanelles and of Turkish positions, probably used for planning gunfire support targets.

Three weeks later another battleship, HMS *Goliath*, was sunk by a torpedo fired by a Turkish destroyer just inside the Straits where she was giving gunfire support to the army. Soon afterwards rumours started to circulate that the Germans were operating submarines in the Aegean Sea. They were confirmed when one of the battleships saw a periscope and fired at it. Destroyers moved in and most of the battleships in the immediate vicinity weighed anchor.

Luckily *Swiftsure*'s crew consisted almost entirely of keen, highly disciplined active service ratings as opposed to most of the old battleships of the Second Fleet which had been made up to strength by drafts of elderly reservists. *Swiftsure*'s crew ran a sweepstake for the person who first saw a periscope and when on 25 May a submarine was sighted gunners got off several rounds at record speed and the enemy disappeared. Soon afterwards a torpedo was fired at another battleship which missed, but then the *Triumph* was hit. *Swiftsure*'s officers watched from the quarterdeck as she rolled over and sank. The admiral then decided to send most of the battleships away from the coast while destroyers conducted a thorough sweep of the area. Only the old *Majestic* remained to give covering fire to the troops. Next day she moved even closer inshore than the troop transports where it was thought that no submarine could get at her, but early the following morning she was torpedoed and sank. Thus six of the thirteen battleships that started the campaign in February were now lost.

Three separate paintings by H.K. designed to be put together as shown in order to denote positions held by both sides from the entrance to the Dardenelles on the extreme right and covering V, W and X beaches.

By July it was clear that the troops that had landed either side of Cape Helles were not going to break through the Turkish defences. It was therefore decided to shift the main effort further north where the Australian and New Zealand forces were fighting. They would be reinforced for a major offensive in August. To assist them an extra army corps would be put ashore on their left flank at Suvla Bay. Once again *Swiftsure* found herself covering the landing and being subjected to heavy fire from the shore. She suffered no major damage but she did suffer a number of casualties. Although the landing succeeded this new offensive did not achieve a breakout despite the extreme gallantry of the soldiers.

The failure of the new offensive and the inability of the army to provide the massive reinforcement thought necessary for it to succeed, resulted in a decision being made to evacuate the Gallipoli Peninsula. Already nearly 100,000 soldiers were tied down there and the problem was to get them out without further loss. It was decided first to clear the troops from the northern area occupied by the 9th Corps, which had landed at Suvla, and the primarily Australian and New Zealand troops fighting alongside them. The last phase of this evacuation was entrusted to the commander of the 9th Corps Lieutenant General Sir Julian Byng whose headquarters was to lie offshore in a sloop. Commander Kitson was attached to Byng's staff for this operation. Contrary to all expectation the Turks were taken by surprise and the evacuation was carried out during the night of 18-19 December without loss of life. A further evacuation of the southern sector around Cape Helles took place 7-8 January and the campaign came to a close, *Swiftsure* returning to England on 7 February.

In a letter to the First Sea Lord regretting the departure of this ship, Admiral de Robeck, the naval Commander-in-Chief, stated that *Swiftsure* had "an exceptionally good ship's

The evacuation of Suvla 9.am Sunday.

Pencil sketch by H.K. depicting the evacuation from Suvla Bay.

company." This must have been largely down to Kitson's influence as the ship's executive officer. For his part in the campaign he received a further mention in despatches. When considering the naval aspects of the campaign it is interesting to notice how much more time the ships of the fleet spent in action than was the case in, for example, the Grand Fleet based at Scapa Flow. Those great ships achieved their object by existing rather than fighting, with the exception of the one big Battle of Jutland, although the battlecruisers at Rosyth were more often in action. The ships in the Dardanelles campaign spent months on end being shelled or subject to the perils of enemy submarines or mines with proportionally large losses of ships and men.

Another matter of minor interest was that in the latter part of 1915 a new type of warship designed for coastal bombardment started to arrive. They were called Monitors and consisted of little more than a floating gun platform fitted with massive torpedo protection in the form of great bulges to the hull. They were slow and ungainly to look at but they each carried large turret-mounted guns capable of firing heavy shells over great distances. Their deployment enabled the battleships to operate in more secure places than had been possible in the early part of the year. In 1916 Kitson took command of the monitor *Marshal Ney* in the Dover Patrol, but after a few months he was promoted to Captain. He then spent a year as Assistant Director of Naval Intelligence in the Admiralty at the end of which he was sent on a mission to the Hague concerned with arranging for an exchange of prisoners of war. Discussions with "our friends the enemy," as he described them in a letter to his father, were complicated. On his return King George V, who took a great interest in the negotiations, called for him to explain how they were going.

HMS Carlisle.

In the last months of the war Captain Kitson was given command of the newly completed cruiser, HMS *Carlisle* in the Grand Fleet. By this time he was acquainted with the celebrated marine artist, Wyllie, who gave him a dry point etching of the *Carlisle* signed W.L. Wyllie to Captain H.K.Kitson. Some years later they were corresponding about how best to send a picture of HMS *Calcutta* to India.

Small pencil sketch of HMS Carlisle.

Dry point etching of HMS Carlisle *by W.L. Wyllie presented to H.K. by the artist.*

Early in 1919 Kitson took over command of HMS *Cornwall* in which cadets on leaving Dartmouth spent time at sea before joining the fleet as midshipmen. Cornwall, a cruiser of 9,800 tons, first commissioned in 1904 and with a main armament of 14 x 6inch guns, had distinguished herself in the Battle of the Falkland Islands in 1914. But now a lot of work at Devonport dockyard was needed to get her clean and ready to take the cadets, and this had to be carried out during a record spell of wet weather; 50 consecutive days of continuous rain. The ship eventually set sail on 4 February.

One of more than 100 paintings of fish caught and catalogued by H.K. during his naval careeer.

The ensuing cruise took them to Gibraltar and the Cape Verde Islands before crossing the Atlantic. During the crossing an abscess developed under one of Kitson's teeth which was so painful that the medical officer was called on to remove it in the absence of a dentist. Kitson remembered the occasion ever afterwards because of the intense and prolonged agony involved, there being no anaesthetic available. After the ships arrival in Trinidad there followed a series of visits to various islands in the Caribbean. These involved him in making a series of official visits to Governors and captains of British and foreign warships. Once the formalities were over there was usually a series of social and sporting events including shooting, fishing, cricket and many lunches and dinners. Whenever time allowed he fished by using rod and line, nets or even explosives in order to catch and paint as many different sorts of fish as possible, carefully recording their measurements, and their Native, English and Scientific names in his journals. The next port of call was Bermuda in early June followed by Nova Scotia. It was here that he met his eldest sister, Edie, who he had not seen since 1907 as she and her husband were working in Canada.

The ship then went on to Newfoundland where Kitson received orders to help police who were being threatened by armed mobs. At one point he had to land a party of bluejackets and marines to disperse them. This task completed, Kitson managed two successful sorties

Hawke's Bay on the north-west coast of Newfoundland.
(Watercolour 13"x9.5")

into the interior to fish for salmon. It was then time to return to Plymouth where they arrived at the end of July, expecting a further cruise with a new lot of cadets. But at this point the admiralty decided that rather than having two cruisers taking cadets to sea, there would be one old battleship taking twice the numbers. *Cornwall* was paid off and Kitson was appointed to command HMS *Centaur* instead.

HMS *Centaur* was a light cruiser, similar to *Carlisle*, and soon after Captain Kitson took command in September 1919 she became for a time the flagship of the 3rd Light Cruiser Squadron commanded by Rear Admiral Sir George Hope, which was part of the Mediterranean fleet. The Commander-in-Chief, Vice Admiral Sir John de Robeck, flying his flag in HMS *Iron Duke*, was also the High Commissioner at Constantinople responsible for implementing the peace treaty agreed between the wartime allies i.e Britain, France, Italy and Greece, and the defeated Turks. In addition he was responsible for affording assistance to those Russians who were still in arms under General Denikin, fighting against the Bolsheviks to the north of the Black Sea. These people were holding a line from Odessa on the coast in the west in a semicircle to the north of the Crimea and on to the coast again beyond Novorossisk in the East. Further to the south in Georgia, was Batum where there was a garrison of British and Indian troops.

HMS Centaur, *Captain Kitson's ship throughout the operations in the eastern Mediterranean and Black Sea, 1919–20.*

Kitson's first task in early November was to visit Odessa to liaise with the British Military Mission that was supporting Denikin's Russian Army of Volunteers as they were called. His purpose was to discover how the fighting was going, and to assess the situation in Odessa itself. To someone unaccustomed to Russian ways it seemed chaotic, but there was no immediate danger of the Reds taking the town. There followed a lengthy cruise during which Admiral Hope visited the ships in different parts of the Black Sea. Between mid November and mid December they visited Odessa, Yalta, Theodosia, Novorossisk and Batum before returning to Constantinople. During this lengthy cruise there was much calling on Allied and Russian leaders and Captain Kitson experienced without enthusiasm the immensely long eating and drinking sessions associated with such activities. As a small, athletic and fit person, now in his early forties, he greatly disliked having to spend hours eating and drinking to excess.

Kitson's next task in January 1920 was to pass through the Suez Canal and pick up Field Marshal Lord Allenby, the High commissioner in Egypt, and his wife and entourage and take them across the Red Sea to Jeddah on a visit to King Hussein of the Hejaz. Hussein was the ruler of the Arabs who had taken part in the revolt against Turkey during the war and was expecting to be accepted as the ruler of all the lands in Arabia formerly part of the Ottoman Empire, with his capital at Damascus. This was what he had been told by the British during the war, but unfortunately Britain had also agreed with France that they should have Syria and there was no way out of this undertaking. It was Allenby's task to break this unwelcome news to the King, which he did on the afternoon of their arrival. Kitson stayed on the ship for this meeting and spent the time setting off two 16lb explosive charges in the harbour to examine the fish that floated to the surface. When Allenby returned he said that the meeting had gone badly and the King was in tears. Soon afterwards the King's son Abdullah appeared and said the King was sorry and they would all meet again next day. This time Kitson accompanied Allenby and there was a spectacular review of Arab mounted troops and an even more spectacular lunch party. On the following day the King invested Allenby, Kitson and one or two others with the Order of Nahda: 1st Class for Allenby and 2nd Class for the others. Then Centaur took Allenby and his entourage across the Red Sea to Port Sudan where there was another parade, this time of Sudanese soldiers, some of whom had fought against us at Omdurman. Allenby then went inland by train.

Viscount Allenby and King Hussein watching the review of mounted troops.

Centaur was now due for a refit in Gibraltar but on the way she was diverted to Lemnos in order to pick up Mr Mackinder and take him to Marseilles. He was High Commissioner to the Russians fighting the Bolsheviks and he was returning to England to recommend the policy that the British Government should take regarding these people. A decision on this matter was long overdue as neither the navy nor the army had any clear direction as to what they should be doing. They were left to their own devices until they were obliged to do something, at which point they were told it was wrong. Kitson had many long talks with him as the ship traversed the Mediterranean and was amazed at the complexity of the political approach to what seemed like a relatively simple problem. After parting with her passenger, *Centaur* went on to Gibraltar for her refit, which lasted until March.

Lunch party with King Hussein.

By 22 March the ship was back at Constantinople where Kitson found that the situation had greatly deteriorated. He was sent to Theodosia, on the eastern side of the Crimea, as Senior Naval Officer for the area. In addition to *Centaur* he had a number of smaller ships under his command. For the next month he dealt with one crisis after another which included evacuating some 700 men from the British Military Mission to the Volunteer Army. At this time Denikin's headquarters at Novorossisk, had to be moved to Sevastopol on the west side of the Crimea. Denikin himself resigned his command and passed through Theodosia on his way to Constantinople. His place was taken by Baron von Wrangel. Kitson received orders from the Commander-in-Chief to do everything possible to prevent the Bolshevik advance, but on no account to use force even though one of the smaller vessels under his command had on one or two occasions been bombed by Red aircraft. The situation in the town of Theodosia became ever more difficult as refugees poured in and the Volunteer Army became increasingly demoralised.

Funeral of the King of Greece attended by Rear Admiral Hope and Captain Kitson representing the Royal Navy.

The Royal Navy had available four battleships and a number of cruisers and smaller craft. In addition to the Commander-in-chief and Rear Admiral Hope in charge of the cruisers there was Rear Admiral Culme-Seymour who was second in command of the fleet. These admirals took it in turns to visit the Senior Naval Officers at Odessa, Sevastopol, Theodosia and Batum to keep abreast of the situation and to help with refugees. At the end of May Centaur was relieved at Theodosia by another cruiser and sailed via Constantinople to Malta where she re-commissioned, that is to say a new crew came out from England and the old crew returned there. The officers did not change.

At the end of June *Centaur* set off for Taranto to pick up Sir Herbert Samuel the new High Commissioner for Palestine who had to be taken to Haifa. This gave Kitson a further opportunity of looking into the mind of a senior politician. By 9 July he was back at Constantinople to find that the British and Indian troops had been evacuated from Batum, leaving only a naval presence to cheer up the Georgians in the face of the advancing Bolsheviks. Kitson was appointed Senior Naval Officer Batum, but the task was less exacting than it had been in Theodosia. Above all there was no Russian Volunteer Army to work with which made life easier. By the end of August 1920 Centaur left Batum and returned

Photo of HMS Centaur *taken from the bridge of the flagship HMS* Iron Duke.

to the Mediterranean, shortly afterwards becoming Admiral Hope's flagship for the second time. Soon afterwards the King of Greece died and Admiral Hope and Captain Kitson represented the Royal Navy at his funeral.

Returning to Constantinople in November, Kitson was ordered to take some Bolshevik prisoners captured by the Volunteer army back to Odessa which was now in Bolshevik hands. They were to be exchanged for some British seamen that had fallen into the hands of the Bolsheviks. The exchange went well and Centaur headed off to Sevastopol to assist in the evacuation of British citizens trying to flee from the advancing Red Army. By the middle of the month, greatly relieved, he left the Black Sea for the last time. During the past year he felt that he was neither fully at war nor properly at peace which was a condition that he had never before encountered or considered. It was a condition well recognised by the armed forces today.

There was one more excitement in store before he handed the ship over to his successor in January 1921. In mid November the famous Greek Prime Minister Venizelos who had been responsible for greatly improving the status and power of his country was forced out of office. His life was in danger and Centaur was sent to escort him as he escaped from the country in his yacht. This operation went well and Centaur spent the last few weeks of the year in and around Malta.

So ended this very exacting and exciting period in Kitson's career. All the missions that he had been directed to undertake in Centaur were related to the chaos resulting from the Great War. He had lived through the pre-war naval expansion, the war itself and its aftermath. There was still some unfinished business in the Eastern Mediterranean as a resurgent Turkey pushed Greece out of its territory, but from Kitson's point of view he would from now on, find himself having to adjust to the problems of peace. For the Royal Navy this meant less money, fewer ships, and a steady reduction in resources.

HMS Queen, *flagship of the Second Fleet.*
(Watercolour 10"x6.5")

HMS King Edward VII *in which H.K. served as first lieutenant and subsequently as commander.*

Bombay harbour painted by H.K. in 1913 when he was commander of HMS Swiftsure.
(Watercolour 10.5"x5")

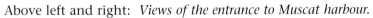

Above left and right: *Views of the entrance to Muscat harbour.*

HMS Swiftsure *before the First World War.*

Newspaper cutting showing HMS Swiftsure. *The caption reads "On to gain fresh glory at the Dardenelles".*

Painting by H.K. of HMS Swiftsure, *before the Dardenelles campaign*
(Watercolour 10.5"x5.5")

Sketch of a merchantman.

HMS Swiftsure under fire entering the Dardenelles on 18 March 1915. This was painted by H.K. long after the event.
(Pastel 23.5"x14.5")

The battlecrusier HMS Indomitable, *sketched by H.K. in 1926 but showing how she appeared in 1916.*
(Charcoal sketch 22"x15")

Light Cruisers at Sea.
(Oil on canvas 23"x12.5")

Pseudoscarus lepidus (parrot fish)

Lutianus aya (red snapper)

Serranidae

Serranidae

A selection of the many fish that H.K. caught and painted during his career. Each watercolour painting measures 13.5"x12.5"

Lutianus sp.

Ship's Company HMS Centaur, *1919. H.K. is seated second row, 6th from left.*

HMS Centaur.

HMS Iron Duke, *painted by H.K. in 1920.*
(Oil on canvas 23.5"x13.25")

The Golden Horn, painted by H.K. in 1920.
(Watercolour 13.5"x7.5")

"A Close Shave."
(Oil on canvas, 1922)

Three pencil sketches from H.K.'s sketchbook.

HMS Barham.

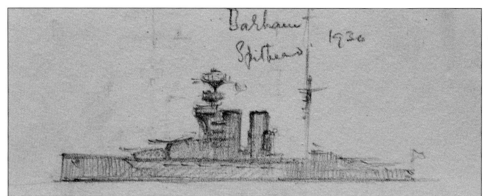

HMS Barham *at Spithead.*

The cruiser HMS Cornwall.

PART 3
1921–1952

Captain Kitson spent the next two years in the Admiralty as Director of the Signals Division, after recovering from a very severe case of blood poisoning. He put his recovery down to the devoted nursing of Sister Agnes in person, at the King Edward VII Hospital in London. He found his time in the Admiralty instructive and his social life enjoyable. In February 1923 he was appointed Flag Captain to Vice Admiral Sir Michael Culme-Seymour, who was shortly to become Commander-in-Chief of the North American and West Indies Station.

One drawback to this posting was that the heavy cruiser HMS *Raleigh*, which should have been the flagship, had been wrecked off Labrador, so the light cruiser, HMS *Calcutta*, was fulfilling the role instead. When the admiral was embarked, together with his wife and daughter, there was little room in the smaller ship for the captain, although things had changed since the days of Jacky Fisher and there was now no need to take horses, a carriage and cows to provide fresh milk. Luckily the admiral and his family spent much of the time ashore at Bermuda. He was also lucky to have as the commander of the ship, Geoffrey Arbuthnott who was a great friend and who had also been his commander in HMS *Cornwall*

HMS Calcutta.

HMS Cornwall - as she later appeared.

The Bermuda coast.
(Watercolour 13"x9")

in 1919. As his navigating officer he had his own brother, Ned, eleven years younger than himself, and by now a lieutenant commander.

Overall Kitson enjoyed the 19 months he spent in this appointment, although from a professional point of view it was not so exacting as his command of *Centaur*. He took over the ship at Bermuda where she stayed until July. During the months spent there he did a lot of painting. In his journal he says "I have never been to any other place where the combination of sea, sky and landscape give such wonderfully rich variations of colour and form. The contrasts also afforded by the dark foliage of the cedar trees and the glimpses of the sea and coral sand combine to make most beautiful pictures everywhere. During the fine periods of the year, September to November and April to July, Bermuda is a painters' paradise." There was also cricket and golf. and he spent time pursuing another of his interests which was identifying the various birds of the island and finding their nests. He also continued to paint and record the many different sorts of fish that he could catch, net or blow up.

In July the ship set out on a cruise to Nova Scotia, Canada and Newfoundland with the admiral and his family embarked. Much of the time was spent calling on Governors of the

Murphy's Falls, Newfoundland.
(Watercolour 9.5"x6.5")

various provinces visited and returning hospitality, but in Newfoundland he found time to re-visit the Salmonier River, which he had first visited when in HMS *Cornwall*. This time fishing conditions were excellent and near Murphy's Falls he caught 23 salmon in one day and a total of 36 over the two days that he was there. On leaving Newfoundland the ship returned briefly to England to re-commission. This time most of the officers remained but some, including his brother, were posted elsewhere. On returning to Bermuda the ship spent a further period there before leaving for a cruise round the West Indies.

In June 1924 the Commander-in-Chief was relieved by Vice Admiral Fergusson. Kitson had got on well with Admiral Culme-Seymour but had found his wife and daughter, though extremely pleasant, to be a great nuisance as they were constantly changing their minds about what they wanted to do. He had become convinced that, as he put it, "a man-of war was no place for a woman," although he greatly enjoyed female company when ashore. Luckily the new admiral did not take his family around with him. Soon after the hand-over, the ship left for another tour of Nova Scotia, Canada and Newfoundland. This time the Salmonier River was too low to fish but a trip to Hawke's Bay towards the northern tip of Newfoundland's west coast proved fruitful. Soon after returning to Bermuda he hand-ed over command of the ship.

Pencil sketch of the eighteenth century HMS Vernon.

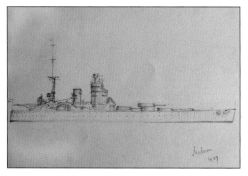

Pencil sketch of HMS Nelson.

Kitson's next appointment was as Captain of HMS *Vernon*, the Royal Navy's Torpedo School. For many years it had operated from a hulk at the top of Portsmouth Harbour, but it had recently moved to the old Gun Wharf just outside the dockyard. Although nearing fifty he was still a fit and good looking man and in 1925 he became engaged to Madge de Pass, fifteen years younger than himself, who he married in 1926. This naturally caused him to regard his time at *Vernon*, where the author of this piece was conceived, with great happiness. His reluctance to having women in ships did not extend to having them ashore. He soon recognised the advantage of having someone as capable and friendly as his new wife to look after the place and organise the hospitality that he was bound to extend to the officers serving in, and visiting, the establishment.

Early in 1927 he heard that he was to become the captain of HMS *Rodney*, a vast new battleship being built at Birkenhead. It would fall to him to carry out sea trials while the ship was manned partly by naval personnel and partly by employees of the builders. In November these trials were complete and the ship was handed over to the Royal Navy and commissioned. At this time the builders, Cammel Laird, presented Kitson with a fine painting of the ship, in appreciation of his conduct during the sea trials. She then sailed to Devonport. *Rodney* and her sister ship *Nelson*, were at the time the largest and most powerful battleships in the world, armed with nine immense 16inch guns and displacing 35,000 tons. Kitson now had to work the ship up so that she could take her place in the fleet. This involved gunnery training and practice with the great 24.5in torpedoes with which the ship was armed. Conducted during the stormy winter months, these trial caused

HMS Rodney.

him much concern but were successfully concluded by the following April. It would be these great guns that thirteen years later helped to smash up the German battleship *Bismarck* after she was damaged by an aerial torpedo and brought to bay, following the destruction of HMS *Hood*. On this occasion *Rodney* even fired a torpedo at the *Bismarck* but missed. This HMS *Rodney* was the fourth ship to carry the name and Kitson painted pictures of three of them to hang in the captain's cabin. Unfortunately these pictures disappeared when the ship was broken up in 1948 and their whereabouts remains unknown.

In April 1928, Kitson was promoted to Rear Admiral and left the *Rodney*: his time in her commemorated in one of the names of his second son. He spent a year on half pay before taking over command of the 3rd Battle Squadron in the Atlantic Fleet. It was to be his last sea-going command. His flagship was HMS *Emperor of India*, a strange coincidence as the first ship he served in, when he went to sea in 1893, was HMS *Empress of India*. Sometimes during his period of command the fleet would join up for exercises designed to test various tactical situations as for example the best formation to employ when in danger of attack from enemy destroyers. At other times individual battle squadrons would take themselves off to carry out gunnery practices or to hold sporting events such as their squadron regattas. Naturally with regard to tactical ideas, there was a split between those who visualised a future naval war as a re-run of the Battle of Jutland and those who thought that the development of naval aviation and undersea operations had already confined such actions to history. As usual the gunnery specialists who were well represented in the senior ranks, favoured the conservative approach, whereas undersea experts, aviators and communicators held more advanced views.

Pencil sketch of the HMS Iron Duke.

The country as a whole was now in the throes of a massive depression, which resulted in vicious cuts in the services. As a result admirals were only allowed a short time in a sea

Far left: HMS Emperor of India. *Left: Pencil sketches of HMS* Emperor of India.

Scottish Loch, 1935.
(Watercolour 10.5"x7.5")

going command so as to give as many as possible the opportunity to get the necessary experience. Thus in 1931 Admiral Kitson found himself appointed as Admiral Superintendent of Portsmouth Dockyard, a post that he occupied for two years as a Rear Admiral and then for two more years as a Vice Admiral. Each year he spent his summer leave with a cousin in the Scottish Highlands fishing and stalking and he took great delight in painting the mountains and sea lochs of that area. He also took part in the Cowes Regattas in his cousin's racing schooner, *Golden Hind*. His last big task in the summer of 1935 was to organise the fleet revue marking King George V's Silver Jubilee. He had recently been knighted and on the day of the review he put to sea in the sloop HMS *Tedworth* with his family and friends to watch this great occasion. Soon afterwards he retired to a house near Farnham, Surrey.

During his years as Admiral Superintendent at Portsmouth, Kitson had further developed his interest in the history of the Royal Navy and of the design of its ships. This lead to him becoming a Vice President of the Navy Records Society and the Society for Nautical Research in which capacity he was closely involved in the setting up of the new maritime museum in the Queen's House at Greenwich. He was directly concerned with the collection and display of pictures, including those of the now dead W.L. Wyllie with whose son

The Golden Hind *schooner belonging to Captain J.B. Kitson, a painting by H.K.*
(Watercolour 8"x8.5")

After the Royal Naval College was built at Dartmouth, Britannia was hulked until being broken up in 1916. This engraving by W.L. Wyllie was presented to Lady Kitson by 'the L:adies of the Dockyard' in September 1935.

Lieutenant Colonel H.L. Wyllie, another distinguished marine artist, he remained in touch. This was a task for which he was very well suited.

Kitson was not left in retirement for long. One evening at the end of June 1940 when a German invasion was thought to be imminent, he was rung up by the Admiralty and told to move to Falmouth, next day if possible, and take charge of the coast of Cornwall in his old rank of Vice Admiral. He had no uniform, having disposed of it when he retired, but he duly arrived in a blue suit to find a headquarters being rapidly assembled and a staff being set up. Initially he did not even have a secretary to type for him until his wife arrived a few days later to fill the gap. Meanwhile the docks and the ships in the harbour were being subjected to sustained air attacks, which in the absence of effective anti aircraft weapons, were devastatingly effective. His hand written record of these early days recounts repeated destruction of docks and neighbouring houses, ships beached and on fire and many men killed and wounded. Later the Germans turned to mining in the bay where large numbers of ships were at anchor. In early August the first searchlights started to arrive and soon the record shows enemy aircraft being shot down, although attacks intensified and at one point the damage was such that the port had to be closed. By the end of September attacks started to ease off.

By this time too the headquarters had been established in a small hotel on the sea front immediately above the dockyard and a house had been found for the Admiral and his family nearby. From the start, although the harbour and dockyard were of major concern, the main part of Kitson's task was to arrange for the proper control of shipping moving through his coastal area. This involved the assembling and despatch of convoys along the south coast and to America. There were also ships moving along the north Cornish coast through the Bristol Channel. When he first arrived there was a great accumulation of vulnerable refugee shipping in Falmouth Bay which had to be dispersed. In addition part of the Royal Netherlands Navy which had escaped at the time of the German assault on that country, were now at anchor in the upper reaches of the Fal estuary and had to be cared for.

Merchantman, pencil sketch.

As time went on matters improved and enemy air attacks concentrated on ships at sea or on laying mines in the approaches to the harbour. None the less the sheer pressure of work and responsibility, particularly in the early months of his appointment, was bound to impose a considerable strain on a man of his age. The fact that he suffered concussion and severe bruising when the blast of a bomb hurled him into a wall was no help. On the other hand he undoubtedly enjoyed returning to life within the naval community, especially as he had a number of his old shipmates working for him. Retired admirals of various sorts, re-employed in the rank of commander had been appointed to the ports of Penzance, Padstow and Fowey as Resident Naval Officers. These were all men he knew well and he certainly enjoyed visiting them. He also had the advantage of being looked after by his wife and a couple of elderly naval reservists in his own house when the days work was done. He may even have enjoyed the company of his two young sons in the school holidays. In the first war his wife had qualified as a Red Cross VAD and had been the Quartermaster of a hospital dealing with men wounded on the western front. Now she was put in charge of the Falmouth Red Cross and spent much time setting up and visiting First Aid Stations to deal with air raid casualties and with injured seamen coming ashore after their ships had been sunk or damaged nearby. Although Kitson had married late in life, he had found a most wonderful wife and mother for his children, with whom he lived in perfect harmony until his dying day.

Vice Admiral Sir Henry and Lady Kitson and their second son Cadet T.E.R. Kitson, at Falmouth, 1942.

In early 1942 the raid against St Nazaire was mounted from Falmouth which turned out to be the last major naval operation in which he would be concerned. Kitson's specialist knowledge of underwater warfare, i.e torpedoes and mines, combined with his experience as Admiral Superintendent of Portsmouth Dockyard had been exactly what was needed at Falmouth. His ability to command, organise and improvise enabled him to put this specialist knowledge to good effect. Throughout his career he had always inspired affection as well as respect, because of his friendliness and because of his ability to impose firm disci-

Vice Admiral Sir Henry and Lady Kitson, with Cadet Kitson, in Devon after leaving Falmouth.

pline without being in the least bit overbearing or unkind. All these qualities helped him through this last great test of his long career. At the end of 1942 at the age of sixty-five he finally retired. It was almost exactly 51 years since as a cadet he had joined HMS *Britannia*, moored in the Dart Estuary.

On leaving Falmouth he went to live near the village of Hennock on the ridge that separates the Rivers Teign and Bovey, a spectacularly beautiful part of Devon, about ten miles from where he was born. Here he painted some of his finest landscapes. At the end of the war with one son in the army and the other in the Royal Navy, he moved back to Surrey where he died in 1952. The writer of his obituary in the Times concluded by saying "His many gifts would have carried him high in the Navy had he reached Flag Rank a few years earlier or later; but nothing could have carried him higher in the affections of his shipmates."

King George VI and Queen Elizabeth inspecting members of the Royal Naval Service at Falmouth in 1942. H.K. is standing to the left of the king.

Above left: *A Thames barge, by H.K.*
(Watercolour 4"x4.5")

Above and left: Depictions of two earlier Rodneys not by H.K. but used by him to paint the set of Rodney pictures given by him to the ship when he left it. The first of the early Rodneys is shown on page 83.

Bombay harbour. A second version of the scene painted by H.K.and shown on page 67.

The Bermuda coastline, a larger painting taken from a similar position to that on page 80.
(Watercolour 13"x10")

Bernuda scene by H.K., 1923
(Watercolour 13.5"x9.5")

At 33,900 tons displacement HMS Rodney, along with her sister ship HMS Nelson, was considered the most powerful battleship afloat at the time of her launching in 1927. These photographs, from H.K.'s albums portray her size and power.

HMS Rodney *with her sister ship, HMS* Nelson, *in the distance, from a painting by H.K.*

Painting by H.K. of a house on the Benacre Estate, Suffolk where the family spent some weeks in the summer of 1930.
(Watercolour 13"x9.5")

A poppy field in Suffolk, painted by H.K. on the Benacre Estate, 1930.
(Watercolour 13"x10")

Scene on the River Tweed where H.K. and his wife spent their honeymoon fishing, and visited on several occasions thereafter.
(Watercolour 9.5"x6.5")

Scottish hillside scene nearby. Probably painted on a Sunday (no fishing!).
(Watercolour 10"x7")

'River Tweed' by H.K., 1928.
(Watercolour 13.5"x9.5")

Left: *Garden of the Admiral Superintendent's House, Portsmouth, painted by H.K. in 1934.*
(Watercolour 10.25"x7.5")

Below: *Street scene adjacent to the Admiral Superintendent's House, Portsmouth, painted by H.K. in 1934.*
(Watercolour 10.5"x8")

A Scottish Sea Loch
(Watercolour 10"x7.5")

A View across Loch Hourn
(Watercolour 11.5"x8.5")

Scottish scene
(Pastel 13"x9.5")

Loch Hourn, 1935.
(Watercolour 12"x8")

A view on the South Downs.
(Watercolour)

Pencil sketch, the frigate Francais.

Pencil sketch, the frigate Juno.

Pencil sketch, the HMS Rodney.

Pencil sketch, the HMS Collingwood.

SOUTH JETTY AND KING'S STAIRS.

A depiction by H.K. of Portsmouth dockyard as in the early days of the nineteenth century.
(Watercolour 12"x8.5")

Vice Admiral Sir Henry Kitson at the 1935 Jubilee Review.

Left and below: *Cadets taken when they joined the navy in 1891 and a reunion dinner of many of the same men in 1936 with H.K. sitting on the front row, left.*

The Second World War cruiser HMS Swiftsure *painted by H.K. in the 1940s to commemorate his time as Commander of her predecessor in the First World War.*
(Pastel 13"x9.5")

Falmouth Bay painted by H.K.in 1947 as a memento of his time at Falmouth 1940–1942 when it looked very different.
(Watercolour 13.5"x9.5")

Southwold Bay, 1935. This is the best of many pictures that H.K. painted of this scene.
(Watercolour 14.5"x10")

A stooked field looking towards Hay Tor, 1944.
(Pastel 12"x8")

Shaptor and view looking towards Lustleigh Cleave.
(Watercolour 14"x9.5")

The field behind the house near Hennock, looking across to Hay Tor on Dartmoor, 1944.
(Watercolour 13"x9.5")